Lineberger Memorial
Library

O let the earth bless the Lord;

O all ye wild, green things upon the earth,

bless ye the Lord, praise him and magnify him forever!

The Green Earth

Poems of Creation

LUCI SHAW

William B. Eerdmans Publishing Company

Grand Rapids, Michigan / Cambridge, U.K.

Wm. B. Eerdmans Publishing Co.

255 Jefferson Ave. S.E., Grand Rapids, Michigan 49503 /

P.O. Box 163, Cambridge CB3 9PU U.K.

www.eerdmans.com

Printed in the United States of America

06 05 04 03 02   5 4 3 2 1

Library of Congress Cataloging-in-Publication Data

Shaw, Luci.

    The green earth: poems of creation / Luci Shaw.

      p.   cm.

    ISBN 0-8028-3942-8 (cloth: alk. paper)

    1. Creation — Poetry. 2. Seasons — Poetry. 3. Poetry — Nature. I. Title.

  PS3569.H384 G74 2002

  811'.54 — dc21

                        2001059224

Images on pages i and 9 © Getty Images; used by permission

Image on page 31 © Corbis; used by permission

Image on page 55 © PhotoDisc; used by permission

This book is for
  Jack Leax, Bob Siegel, and
    Jeanne Murray Walker

Contents

Introduction: The Need to Pay Attention   1

1   Early Green

How to paint a promise in January   11

Heart Spring   12

Forecast   14

Highway Song for Valentine's Day   15

What secret purple wisdom   17

Rising: The Underground Tree   18

April   19

Inscriptions   20

Enthusiasm: The Woods in Spring   23

Spring song, very early morning   24

Bare roofs   26

Folio   27

The Herb Garden   28

Edges of Wales   29

2   **Summer Green**

In my living room   33

Benediction: Opening the Summer Cottage   34

A Song for Simplicity   36

Showers in the Foothills   38

Windy   39

Soft   40

Flathead Lake, Montana   42

Imprints: Lindisfarne   43

Forest Green   44

I begin to understand how weather   45

Raining   46

Three Haiku: Queen Anne's Lace   47

Raspberries   48

Weather Forecast: Prolonged Dry Period   49

Stigmata   50

On the river bank, Bibury   51

Grass   52

3 Green to Gold

Diamonds that leap   57

The Meaning of White Oaks   58

Villanelle for a season's ending   60

Harvesting   61

Benedictus   62

Evaporation   63

The Writing on the Rock   64

Bone Creek   65

Overleaf   67

Materfamilias   68

Mobile   69

Golden Delicious   70

M. C. Escher's Three Worlds   71

Behind the walls   73

What the wind can do   74

To a Winter Chestnut: Five Haiku   75

I gave this day to God   76

Introduction: The Need to Pay Attention

"Nobody sees a flower, really — it is so small —
we haven't time . . ."

Georgia O'Keeffe

"If your heart is straight with God, then every creature will
be to you a mirror of life and a book of holy doctrine."

Thomas à Kempis, *Imitatio Christi*

"Don't you get tired of *noticing* things?" The question was leveled at me like a small pebble from a sling. The student in the lecture hall seemed to be irritated. My hunch was that something in my poetry had unsettled her, and she was getting back at me during the question-and-answer time after the poetry reading.

By way of answering her, I quoted one of my favorite sayings from Annie Dillard, embodied in a brief essay she wrote for *Life* magazine on, of all things, "The Meaning of Life": "We are here to abet Creation and to witness it, to notice each thing, so each thing gets noticed . . . so that Creation need not play to an empty house." Dillard also says, in *Pilgrim at Tinker Creek,* "Beauty and Grace are performed whether or not we sense them. The least we can do is try to be there."

We cannot consume a six-course dinner in one gulp; to enjoy a meal to its fullest, we must savor every bite one flavorful morsel at a time. Nor can we take in the whole universe at once. Every day gives us new chances for small discoveries, ways to view some commonplace object from a fresh angle, to acknowledge what Duns Scotus called *haeccitas,* the "this-ness," the "is-ness," of things, to recognize what we already know but still need to learn, to detect the extraordinary in the ordinary. A move in the direction of this kind of awareness is a move toward a fresh appreciation of our richly detailed universe — the Creator's handiwork. The prime motivation for this exercise is curiosity; the prime requisites are time and focused attentiveness.

Recently I returned from a two-and-a-half week trip to the South Island of New Zealand, a land almost as unspoiled and uncongested as Eden. Most of the time I was alone, with camera and journal, intentionally opening my mental pores, as it were, to sensations and impressions. Here's a journal entry I wrote during some days I spent in the subtropical rain forest of the west coast:

"True gratitude requires a concentrated awareness, a single eye, which is linked to recognition. Awareness, attentiveness is something we all need to learn, or re-learn, and practice. Both these A-words are linked with our ability to see. When we take the time, we find a kind of exhilaration in small things. My camera lens, with its zoom magnification, helps me to scrutinize what I might otherwise merely glance at and move on. It becomes my other eye. When I frame and focus, I am also focusing my brain.

"Here in the lushness of the rain forest I notice the microcosm of the moss gardens — minute, damp, velvet fronds like green sea anemones — small, low, unknown, unnamed greens. Green upon green upon green, lavish, even wanton in its rich diversity and texture. Diminutive starflowers scattered among the path-side grasses. Tiny, uniformly polished and rounded stream pebbles, all the same shade of gray. The lacy, almost inky foliage of the New Zealand black birches.

"My slowing down, stopping, being still, listening, allows me to hear the microcosm speak — the world of negligible, unnoticed things. We don't need to be world travelers or theologians or philosophers or ecologists in order to see, and hear, the messages of heaven in the earthly creation.

"My pleasure in this was so intense that it brought its own species of frustration. My regret was, 'So much rain forest; so little time.' For us to have a working world which functions efficiently, in which natural processes interact to reproduce and control healthy life, would seem, to a human perspective, quite enough to expect from the Creator. So why is there such a profusion of species? Why the rich complexity and intricacy? Why pattern, and the full spectrum of colors? God is, like all poets, an experimenter, adding the grace of *beauty*, something non-essential in a pragmatic sense, but a clear reflection of what theologians call Grace. And each of us has a flash of that same aesthetic impulse, which needs only a modicum of human cultivation and expression to make us appreciative of the idiosyncrasies and surprises around us, and send us off in our own creative directions.

"We tend to think of the Creator in terms of the infinitely huge — mountains, continents, oceans, galaxies, universes, light-years. As the Almighty is beyond gender and time, so is he beyond size, glimpsed, if we open our eyes, in minor, unpretentious phenomena — the helical unfolding of a shell, the lace of veins in a leaf with sunlight behind it, or, as we penetrate deeper into physical realities, in the structures of subatomic particles and in the endless unfolding of fractal patterns." We see this concentration of limitlessness within limitation in the Incarnation, in Almighty God clothed in a human body, a human life.

And now, the reason for this book, this series of reflections. A poem is a little lens through which we can examine at close range some of the "insignificant" details of the universe, a miniature window on the world. In such small works of art the poet is lending you, the reader, her eyes in hopes that your own eyes will be captivated by things you've never noticed before.

These poems, drawn from different times and places in my life, are all intensely personal, and my hope is that as you read and absorb them, they will become part of your vivid personal experience. It is helpful to remember that in literary poetry there is often some enigma; as Robert Frost observed, "A poem that is completely clear is a trifle glaring." What this means is that as poetry is read aloud, thoughtfully, allowing time and repeated readings to open up layers of meaning within the written lines, the reader's creative imagination must also come alive, becoming almost as vital a part of the process as the artistic intent of the poet. And every reader will make something different of a poem as it is interpreted in light of a life that is unique to each.

I am often asked, "How does a poem happen?" This is a mystery, but usually I find myself stirred by the sudden (and often inconvenient) arrival of an image, or an idea, or a resonant phrase that will not leave me alone. I may be preparing dinner for eight, or be shopping in the vegetable section of the supermarket, but this imperious idea will not be denied. It demands that I pay attention. Sometimes this begins when I read another poet's evocative work. The spark of an image kindles my own imagination and I am off, like a startled animal. At this point I am not quite responsible for my own actions. Preoccupied, I may break an egg into the garbage disposal, or absentmindedly put a pot of hot coffee in the refrigerator. I suppose this is what makes a poet a poet — that slender antenna of awareness that is always extended, combing the air for images, listening to the rhythms of language, watching, noticing when something quite unremarkable achieves a significance that cries out to be crafted into an art form.

Poetry is both an art and a craft. The art lies in the recognition that something has potential as a poem. But the craft, the polishing of the poem on the page, or the computer screen, often takes dozens of rewrites over months or years. A poem I wrote twenty-five years ago, which had lain unfinished, waiting like an embryo in a file folder, just recently came alive for me as I found an image and a phrase that completed it and allowed it to be born.

The greenness and earthiness of the world has always moved me — its fertility, its self-renewal. Summer holidays with my family in Muskoka, Ontario, gave me experiences that I remember like good dreams. Drifting in a canoe along a lakeshore, shadowed by firs and cedars, collecting the green velvet hillocks of moss on the boulders, bringing them back to our cottage and forming with them — and twigs and lichens and pebbles — a miniature landscape in a metal cookie tin to keep the dream of green alive. The memory of camping on the shores of Georgian Bay informs my notions of wind and rock. Old photographs of canoe trips on the Mary River and Mary Lake bring to mind the reflected colors of sky and verdant shore and those primal islands and forests. It all reinforces the dream and refreshes the mind's fertility. Memory and imagination work well together.

My books of poetry — especially *Listen to the Green*, *The Secret Trees*, and *Writing the River* — extend the metaphors of green and flowing, growing things.

Where I live now, in the Pacific Northwest, my study window opens onto a deep ravine guarded by cedars and banked with sword ferns above a stream that sends its sounds into my thoughts and my writing. I tell people, "I write best to the sound of running water." The shore of any ocean has much the same effect on me: its limitlessness, the borders of air and land and water rubbing at each other, the random treasures to be found and collected along the tide lines — many of these end up in poems. I catch myself saying — as I follow the edges of the incoming waves, and pick up a pebble here, a shell there, an aqua winking eye of sea glass, a knot of driftwood — "This is the state of happiness. This is my purest happiness." And when a poem has become itself, when it feels complete and I know that further revision will only muddy it, I echo Dorothy Sayers, who could say, on finishing a novel (or an essay, or a poem), "I feel like God on the Seventh Day!"

1 *Early Green*

How to paint a promise in January

for Lauren

Here in my winter breakfast room
the colors of rainbows are
reduced to eight solid lozenges in a
white metal tray. A child's brush
muddies them to gray in a
glass of water. Even the light breaks down
as it pushes through the rain-streaked
windows and polishes the wooden table
imperfectly.
      Green leaves always turn
brown. Summer died into the dark days
a long time ago; it is hard even to
remember what it was like, stalled
as I am in this narrow slot of time
and daylight.
      Until I look down again
and see, puddling along the paper,
under a painted orange sun
primitive as the first spoked wheel,
the ribbon of color flowing out of
my grand-daughter's memory — a new
rainbow, arc-ing wet over strokes of grass
green enough to be true.

Heart Spring

Often, even before Easter,
last summer's deep
seeds rebel
at their long frozen sleep,
split, swell
in the dark under
ground, twist, dance
to a new beat,
push through a lace of old
pale roots.

Invited by an unseen heat
they spearhead up, almost
as though, suddenly,
their tender shoots
find the loam light as air,
not dense, not sodden cold.

I saw a crocus once
in first flight
stretching so fast
from a late snow
(a boundary just passed,
a singular horizon close below)
the white cap melted
on its purple head.

Such swift greening of
leaf wings and stalk
was clear celebration
of all sweet springs combined,
of sungold,
smell of freshness, wind
first-time felt,
light lifting, all new things,
all things good and right,
and all the old
left behind.

Forecast

planting seeds
inevitably
changes my feelings
about rain

Highway Song for Valentine's Day

"Kim, I love you — Danny"
                                   roadside graffito

On overhead and underpass,
beside the road, beyond the grass,

in aerosol or paint or chalk
the stones cry out, the billboards talk.

On rock and wall and bridge and tree,
boldly engraved for all to see,

hearts and initials intertwine
their passionate, short-lived valentine.

I'm listening for a longer Lover
whose declaration lasts forever:

from field and flower, through wind and breath,
in straw and star, by birth and death,

his urgent language of desire
flickers in dew and frost and fire.

This earliest spring that I have seen
shows me that tender love in green,

and on my windshield, clear and plain,
my Dearest signs his name in rain.

What secret purple wisdom

What word informs the world,
and moves the worm along in his blind tunnel?

What secret purple wisdom tells the iris edges
to unfold in frills? What juiced and emerald thrill

urges the sap until the bud resolves
its tight riddle? What irresistible command

unfurls *this* cloud above *this* greening hill,
or one more wave — its spreading foam and foil —

across the flats of sand? What minor thrust
of energy issues up from humus in a froth

of ferns? Delicate as a laser, it filigrees
the snow, the stars. Listen close — What silver sound

thaws winter into spring? Speaks clamor into singing?
Gives love for loneliness? It is this

un-terrestrial pulse, deep as heaven, that folds you
in its tingling embrace, gongs in your echo heart.

Rising: The Underground Tree

(Cornus sanguinea and cornus canadensis)

One spring in Tennessee I walked a tunnel
under dogwood trees, noting the petals
(in fours like crosses) and at each tender apex
four russet stains dark as Christ-wounds.
I knew that with the year the dogwood flower heads
would ripen into berry clusters bright as drops of gore.

Last week, a double-click on Botany
startled me with the kinship of those trees
and bunchberries, whose densely crowded mat
carpets the deep woods around my valley cabin.
Only their flowers — those white quartets of petals —
suggest the blood relationship. Since then I see

the miniature leaves and buds as tips of trees
burgeoning underground, knotted roots like limbs
pushing up to light through rock and humus.
The pure cross-flowers at my feet redeem
their long, dark burial in the ground, show how even
a weight of stony soil cannot keep Easter at bay.

April

The air is filled with south —
Breath which though soft, unseen,
Pants warm from some far tropic mouth
And mists the world with green.

Inscriptions

All this spring, I've worn dirt
under my fingernails like a label —
little black moons.

My garden imprints me:
the stubborn slime of slug;
the invisible prick of a minor thorn
in the pink flesh of the fingertip;
the tomato-plant smell
that clings to my green fingers
for hours, scenting my salads;
the mud that clumps into my house
along with me (I see my footprints
on the burnished tiles of all
my hallways).

The branding burns both ways.
For three years, observing
the old decree to replenish
and subdue, I have been
reshaping this small Eden,
from a bare, primal clay
embedded with gravel
and construction debris

to this riot, this rich boil of blues
and mauves, yellows, creams,
variegated greens. I cultivate,
fertilize, plant, prune, pluck,
import ladybugs to combat
the pale jade scabs of aphids
on the lupine stems. I train
the flow of sapphire clematis up
its trellis, espalier a small apple tree,
rub my astonished eyes at
blooming pinks and fuchsias;
did the colors lend their names
to flowers, or flowers to these
brilliant intensities? I pull and
discard handfuls of kaleidoscopic
weeds, their leaves all intricate
foliate design, their flyaway seeds
wonders of procreation.
"Perennials naturalize,"
says a knowing friend. "Weeds
simply spread, like sin."

This April afternoon,
I glared into the furtive eyes of two
adolescent deer just up from
the ravine on their stick legs,

nibbling larkspurs and peonies
clear down to their roots. Their glance
interrogated me, alarmed:
"Did we do something wrong?" "Go!"
I shouted. "Get out of my garden!"

After this, inscribed as I am
by both offense and grace, will I
ever see gardening, and the Garden,
quite the same way again?

Enthusiasm: The Woods in Spring

A dull day. The earth track through the scrim of trees
unrolls like a faded ribbon. But to the left,
to the right, the woods are swollen with life,
sap rising, the earth exploding, bushes bursting with
an extravagant vigor. Green spurts from every
notch and knot, stems take color (having rebelled
at their strict winter uniform of gray); after drinking rain
all winter, canes and brambles, gravid with juice,
garnish the exuberant air with twigs in cinnamon,
snuff, rose, saffron, bronze, chestnut — rampant,
an intricate etching. Even the spaces between are thick
with desire. Light shines from the cells of leaves like
little suns. Under a pewter sky all the green is neon.

A sheaf of pussy willow clutched in my hands seems
to be growing from the ends of my arm bones. My face
glows with reflected colors of leaves. My feet root
in the sod. An illusion? But a small, emerald voice declares
in the undergrowth: "Cut me back? Like you, I'll spring up
from the ground to crowd the air again, irrepressible."

Spring song, very early morning

All the field's a hymn! All
dandelions give glory, gold
and silver. All trilliums unfold
white flames above their trinities
of leaves. All wild strawberries
and massed wood violets reflect the skies'
clean blue and white.
All brambles, all daisies,
all stalks and stems lift to the light.
All young windflower bells
tremble on hair
springs in the bright air's
carillon touch. Last year's yarrow
(raising brittle star skeletons)
tells: age is not past praising.
All small, low, unknown,
unnamed weeds
show their impossible greens.
All grasses sing,
tone on clear tone.
All mosses spread a spring-
soft velvet for our feet,
and by all means
all leaves, buds, flowers cup

jewels of fire and ice
holding up
to this kind morning's heat
their silver sacrifice.

Bare roofs

Against the sky their angles lean.
Their straight, steep pitch is rarely green.
A metaphor is plainly seen:

The roofs will not accept the rain;
they let it run away again
into the gutters, down the drain,

showing the trees a splendid sheen.
It does not do to be too clean
if you have dreams of growing green.

Folio

Flattened like coins on train tracks,
the *prunus* leaves unfurl along their twigs
in copper ovals. She bends down,
peers in. Shadowed underneath,
each leaf greens in its
charcoal dark, laced with veins
rosy as human arterial blood, delicate
as her own most minor capillaries.

Here are two secrets: the bud
bursting pink from the groin where
leaf stem embraces branch; the curled worm
slung in its pale cocoon, waiting.

Here is another: she has walked around
all day, feeling raw as that bloody leaf,
or worse, a blank page. Priceless
as a flat penny, she'll end up
shriveled for sure, food for the worm.
Against the odds, maybe she'll bloom first.

The Herb Garden

Like this one, some poems are written with a plan in mind —
fourteen lines like a plowed patch cut in rectangles — eight and six
parallel furrows — spaced by a frame of grass borders. Stakes
impaling the empty herb packets mark each strip's end,
echoing each other in a vegetable rhyme for the eye.
Over time this all grows to a patterned satisfaction — a pleasure
at the exuberant pushing up of a vernal brocade
into our field of vision — sage, thyme, arugula, lavender, dill.

The miniature plot, seen from this second-floor window, is compact
as a scrap of fabric. Up here the woman who gardens
manages her square of needlework. She is so amazed! Fertile as her own
imagination (open to the tints of air, spring, sun, and the stabbing
needles of rain), the colored shapes show up, stitch by stitch under
her fingers — green covering brown, a spreading embroidery of leaves.

Edges of Wales

Stalking the blind lanes, striding to the hill
top before daybreak, often I've ached at the sweet chill
of spring light glittering through an intricacy
of leaves, when, in its precision of green, every tree
turns candle. With a series of airy, sharp surprises
crow's wings fold pearly heaven. Then the full sun rises,
polishing the view — stones quick and wet as steel,
glitter on a cobweb, gravel under my heel.

But on *this* early day in May, I wake
through light opaque as milk. The hedgerows make
mysteries with the mist. The cries of sheep shiver
the drenched air. Like silk sliding away, the river
moves south, the sheen of its crease
supple between banks and bushes blanched as fleece.
I thought I loved the hard, bright edges best
until I melted in this morning's mist.

2 Summer Green

In my living room

I have a carpet, green as outside grass.
Its short, dense, woolly blades all seem to wait
for the old Hoover to mow down the dirt
and rake dead fibers, miscellaneous leaves
of lint, into itself. I almost wish
the rain would pour down from the ceilinged sky,
silver and fresh, onto this inside lawn.
Then from the hanging corner globe, switched on
(sun breaking through after the shower's over),
a flood of yellow sunlight might bewitch
a robin into pulling at a worm
daring to tunnel the close woven sod.

Benediction: Opening the Summer Cottage

We stop by the roadside on the way in
to pick daisies, feathered grass heads,
the magenta flame of fireweed.

Unpacking, we settle in for the month:
Oiling the squeaky screen door, sweeping up
dead flies and mouse droppings (a mouse

has grown a family in the sofa). Through
opened windows the fields breathe
into the musty bedrooms.

I fill my aunt's old washer —
fly-specked linen and tea towels with
mysterious stains — run the wet cloth

through the mangle, water in little rivers
down my arms all the way out to the line
and later in the afternoon

I pull the stiff tablecloth out of the sky
to cape a table and scent the kitchen
with its metallic incense.

Sliced tomatoes from the farm stand —
sprinkled with brown sugar, salt, vinegar —
they sluice our tongues with summer juice

at the end of the first day. The wildflowers
in the jam jar say the blessing for us
before supper.

"Create in me a clean heart, O Lord . . ."

A Song for Simplicity

There are some things that should be as they are:
plain, unadorned, common, and all-complete;
things not in a clutter, not in a clump,
unmuddled and unmeddled with,
the straight, the smooth, the salt, the sour, the sweet.
For all that's timeless, untutored, untailored, and untooled,
for innocence unschooled,
for unplowed prairie, primal snow and sod,
water unmuddied, wind unruled,
for these, thank God.

With both hands unjewelled and with unbound hair
beauty herself stands unselfconscious where
she is enough to have, and worth the always holding.
The mind perceiving her, the heart enfolding
echoes the unchanged pattern from above
that praises God for loveliness, and love.

Glory again to God for word and phrase
whose magic, matching the mind's computed leap,
lands on the lip of truth
(plain as a stone well's mouth, and just as deep),
and for the drum, the bell, the flute, the harp, the bird,
for music, *Praise!* that speaks without a word.

As for the rightness to be found
in the unembellished square, and the plain round,
in geometric statement of a curve,
respond without reserve
but with astonishment that there's for every woman,
every man,
one point in time, one plainly drafted plan.
And in your unique place
give glory for God's grace!

All this from Him whose three-in-one
so simply brought to birth
from the red earth
a son.
All our complexity, diversity, decor,
facet the gem, encrust the clarity.
So pierce we now the opalescent glaze
till all our praise
rises to Him in whom we find no flaw.

Showers in the Foothills

Perhaps it takes a thunderstorm for me
    to hear the song of showers. I am a tree.

The clear rain pebbles touch each coin of
    my leafy greenness like a piano key.

Below, then, clouds and sky begin to shine
    from pools and puddles as the falling line

of rain — the complication of the torrent —
    moves off. Storm flinches, then abates, is spent,

is simplified into its glossiest sheen,
    leaves only music singing from the green.

Windy

The maple seeds have spent themselves;
their wings lie mute and brown and tattered
along the grass. The peonies
have let their bloodied white be scattered,
and all this windy afternoon
I've grieved as if it really mattered.

Soft

. . . have a little pity for
every soft thing . . .

                    Mary Oliver

I am one of the soft things
that walks around the world,
open, unguarded. I enter
the green, weeping cloud —
the tent the pepper-berry tree makes
of her foliage — and feel at home.
I keep company with the bodies
of rabbits and bees. I relish the tender
flesh of tomatoes, inviting bruises
under their polished skins,
and the tender flush of the clematis
just opening its face to the sun for
the first time, exposing the nakedness
of innocence, not having felt the sting
of snow yet, or the slow sword of frost.

Eyeballs are such delicate gel;
the blink of the eye may not be
quick enough. The ear,
with its pliable pink cartilage,

the nose likewise, its hidden passages
guarded by a garrison of fine hairs
trembling in the surge of breath.
The crushable mouth and its secret —
the enclosed spatula of tongue,
unsheathed only for talk, taste,
and kiss. My fingertip jerks back
from the quick burn of a surface
unless calluses thicken into
a numbness like armor.

My heart has its soft membranes, too,
easily breached. But know this:
it is better to have a heart that can break
than a leaden stone in the chest,
implacable, weighing down
your whole body, your soul.

Flathead Lake, Montana

"Christ plays in ten thousand places."
                                    Gerard Manley Hopkins

Lying here on the short grass, I am
a bowl for sunlight.

Silence. A bee. The lip lip of water
over stones. The swish and slap, hollow

under the dock. Down-shore
a man sawing wood.

Christ in the sunshine laughing
through the green translucent wings

of maple seeds. A bird
resting its song on two notes.

Imprints: Lindisfarne

I

Here the slow tongue of sea licks at the English coast,
    glazing the shingle — a shallow tray of pebbles —

with its salt saliva. The road stretching out to Holy Island
    hops with hard rain, drowns in the tide

twice a day as Lindisfarne cuts herself off,
    achieves her separation and retreat.

II

Around the Abbey, wind has eaten the faces of angels, carved
    the columned sandstone to abstraction. In the neighbor church

the stained glass is grimed with candle wax,
    old prayers have varnished the arches with their incense,

and on the low plant by the door, a snail is pressing its wet kiss,
    blessing the green with morning silver.

Forest Green

For centuries now the old-growth forest,
a victim, but also a devourer of the world,
has pulled into its slow boil of seasons,
into its emerald mouth beyond the hills, the sky's
gold light, the elements of air, the sacred fluids —
creeks, rains, winter fogs — trapping clouds
of flying seeds, requiring the death of leaves
for a humus rich and dark as old leather,
rotting in small clumps the bones of birds,
translating all this fleshy language,
holding its secret meanings in a net
of vines and roots. The forest keeps on writing
its own narrative in flourishes of green ink.

I begin to understand how weather

The wet gusts that all yesterday afternoon
swept our mountains with their gray silk
skirts — their cold cloth rinsed our faces —

have calmed and recombined tonight
in the placid lake that gleams below our window.
It shows its stormy origins —

ripples fretted like clouds, and liquid light
glancing from an awkward moon that stares,
double-faced, from sky, from water. I begin

to understand how weather — like verse, like
memory, like love — plays with pieces of the past,
makes new of old, festoons bare twigs with

jewels. From God knows where,
miracles come. And for you I am making
this green blessing from fallen rain.

Raining

Like spun silk, water strives
to find its end, a fluid form.
It shapes itself to multitudes of leaves
and riverbeds, and overhanging eaves.

Gravity pulls the silver down,
a liquid tent around the cabin porch,
with filaments like fishing lines. Ropes
of glass beads with their shining drops —

each singing its own syncopated sound
into the pail we set to catch the drips —
have raised the level so the pitch
climbs higher every hour, in the round

tin bucket, till it's full up to the brim.
Like rain or sorrow, love takes its time
to name its music
or to find a rhyme.

Three Haiku: Queen Anne's Lace

It lifts its lovely,
loose exactness — like fireworks,
outstarrings of God.

Cut, it rebels at
the constriction of a vase,
foams into the dark.

Its small galaxy
traces a powder of stars
on the polished wood.

Raspberries

Robins and chickadees, quick
as scissors, are there first,
sighting along the hairy stems,
slanting under leaves, darting
between thorns to the hearts,
pendant as jewels.

The birds think the berries theirs

and us the shameless thieves.
Our human neighbor, too, is adversarial.
Always the primitive growth threatens
to prickle into his acre. Last May
he fired our canes (while we were gone),
not knowing you can't get rid
of raspberries that way. Up
from their small holocaust
they grew back twice as thick.

Today, undaunted by the scowl
from next door, I hunker down, squinting
against the sun, lifting aside the leaves,
plunging my whole arm to a bush's heart,
my skin crossed with beaded wires
of blood, my palms bright with
a sweet serum. Thinking thorns, and blood,
and fruit, I take into my fingers,
bit by bit, the sum of summer.

Weather Forecast: Prolonged Dry Period

The cattle who should, according
to folklore, be lying down at the approach of rain,
stand skeptical in a field of ragged green. The sky,
a surging pewter, exhibits a tatter of gulls.

Like cows, I live under a conditional heaven;
clouds keep tearing apart, then mending,
heavy with partial images. Moments ago
a sheaf of rain, weighted with promise, breached

the foothills. Now its silver ghost
breasts the cow pasture, looms closer, then passes
barely a hundred yards to my left. It
never even blesses my forehead with its fierce

mist. In tune with the random weather,
its errors of judgment, I wait. But for what?
A wind from the south? A green
perfection? A seven-year drought?

The forecaster preaches his dogma, predicting
high pressure as long and irritating as intractable optimism.
He may prove wrong. I long to be soaked through.
I want it to pour, relentless, for weeks.

Stigmata

The tree, a beech, casts the
melancholy of shadow across the road.
It seems to bear the enormous weight of
the sky on the tips of its branches.
The smooth trunk invites me to finger

five bruise-dark holes where rot
was cut away. Years have pursed
the thickened skin around the scars
into mouths that sigh,
"Wounded. Wounded."

As the hurt feels me out,
wind possesses the tree and
overhead a hush comes; not that
all other sounds die, but half a million
beech leaves rub together in the air,

washing out bird calls, footsteps,
filling my ears with the memory of
old pain and a song of cells in the sun.
"Hush," they say with green lips.
"Hush."

On the river bank, Bibury

Why do you suddenly ask me am I happy?
I am only combing my mind, like water
searching the green weed. Under the plane
tree, in this confusion of suns, crescent

trout flip their golden spines
into the air, then straighten,
heads upstream, in the clear path of water.
I know now it is their bliss to be still

in a current. The grassy fringes between glare
and dusk teach them how a river bank
casts a shadow of rest; how fixed and tranquil
lie the dark stones at river bottom.

Grass

"All flesh is grass,"
and I can feel myself growing
an inch an hour in the dark,
ornamented with a lyric dew
fine as glass beads, my edges
thin as green hair.

All flesh — and there are
seventeen kinds of us
in this one corner of the
hayfield, along with clover,
oxalis, chicory, Wild Wilbur —
close enough cousins for
a succulent hay.

Early mornings
we all smell of rain
enough to drown the microscopic
hoppers and lubricate snails
along their glistening paths:
a fine, wet fragrance, but not
so sweet as this evening, after
the noon scythe.

No longer, now,
are the windows of air
hung with our lace, embroidered
with bees. Laid low, we raise
a new incense, and under
the brief stubble
our roots grieve.

3 Green to Gold

Diamonds that leap

When the leaf fell and brushed my hand
I began to reverse the world. I asked:
What if this warped willow leaf, yellow,

scaled with age, could smooth
to a green blade, then flicker into
the knot of a spring twig, like

a grass snake's tail disappearing, slick
and chill, into his home? That one question —
it was a whirlpool, pulling in

others: What about a river?
Might its waters rush up these indigo
hills of Shenandoah and split to a scatter

of diamonds that leap to their rain
clouds, homing? Can a love
shrink back and back to like,

then to the crack of a small, investigative
smile? Could God ever suck away creation
into his mouth, like a word regretted,
and start us over?

Or this: Can anyone enter the mother's womb
and be born, again?

The Meaning of White Oaks

It is light that tugs,
that teaches each
acorn to defy the pull
down, to interrupt
horizontal space.
And falling, filtering
through the pale green leaves,
it is rain that rises,
then, like a spring
at a sapling's heart.
It is wind that trains,
toughens the wood.
It is time that spreads
the grain in rings —
dark ripples in
a slow pond.

The oaks learn slowly,
well, twisting
up, around, and out,
finding the
new directions of
the old pattern branded
in each branch,

compacting, a wood
dense enough for us
to craft into a crib
for a newborn, a floor
for dancing, a table
for bread and wine,
a door to open,
welcoming daylight.

Villanelle for a season's ending

Autumn is here, and summer will not stay.
The season cuts a bloodline on the land,
And all earth's singing green is stripped away.

Your leaving drains the color from the day.
The oak leaves' red is clotting in my hand.
Autumn is here, and summer will not stay.

The sea fog settles. Even noon is gray.
The light recedes as though this dusk were planned.
The green of field and tree has slipped away.

I shiver on the beach and watch the way
The berries' blood is spilled along the sand.
Autumn is here, and summer will not stay.

In the chill air the knotted weed heads sway.
The waves have swept your footprints from the sand.
The green of all our fields is stripped away.

See how the wind has scattered the salt hay
Across the dunes! Too well I understand:
Autumn is here, bright summer will not stay,
And all earth's love and green are stripped away.

Harvesting

Yesterday, after first frost, with maples
blazing beyond fringes of stubble hay,
my husband and my sons
pulled up dead summer's stalks of corn,
laying them flat among the weeds
for plowing in again, when next spring's born.

I'm glad I picked the green tomatoes
two nights ago
and spread them, newspapered,
to ripen on the basement floor,
good company for the corn relish, row
and golden row in jars behind the pantry door.

Yes, I'm very glad
something's left — something not dead
after all the hilling and hoeing,
seeding and sprouting, greening and growing,
after the blowing
tassels high as a woman's hands above her head.

Let me leave fruit
(but not in someone's basement)
when I grow browned
and old and pulled up by the root
and laid down flat
and plowed into the ground.

Benedictus

When a tree is topped
for the power lines,
the emptiness afterwards is
inhabited by a green
throb of leaves.

Like the vividness we feel about
someone just dead,
the gap
shivers with presence.

Evaporation

Twenty years ago the green square beyond
our back door was webbed with lines
on which I hung with wooden pegs
my angels and my ghosts — white nightgowns
winged in the wind, shrouds of tablecloths,
shirts fluting their spooky sleeves, their
dwindling tails — shadows of the lucid cloth
moving like water on the grass.

Now we live over a basement dryer churning
beneath a 40-watt bulb. The trap keeps filling
with a gray lint as my clothes, my second skins,
are dried out by the dialed minute.
The air behind the house is empty
of apparitions, epiphanies. Gone
is the iron-fresh smell of damp linens
praying their vapor to the sun.

The Writing on the Rock

The morning opens, blue as innocence, over
a lake between granite shores, the old rocks
ribboned with intrusions of quartz.
For eons you northern stones
have spread your ancient pages for
a vermilion scribble of spores,
lichens illegible as lace, a murmur
of olive mosses spelling out
their microscopic struggles for foothold.

But where acid rain gnaws at the boulders
disease spreads its scabs, brittle as dust
under our fingers. Our gift to you — a silver rain
with a bitter bite. You give back what you can —
this delicate embroidery in black. I write
my journal notes; you draft your own slow chronicle
in a dialect of ruin. Tell me, has it healed anything
that some zealot has scrawled across your cliff face,
in white letters large and stark as death, "Jesus Saves"?

Bone Creek

Country road from Sumas

I was startled by sound of it; the name,
it caught me by surprise from the sign
next to the little wooden bridge. "Bone Creek."
I knew, later, as I wrote them into my journal,
something must lie behind the two assertive
syllables; they spoke a sturdy simplicity,
bold-faced, and naïve, like
the unabashed announcement of a crime.

Intrigued by the words' sound,
I stopped the car to hear the voice —
the creek's thin, silver pitch of liquid through
a green field — and wondered about *bone:* Had the
farmer found the ribs of an ox staring whitely
up at him from the stony bottom,
or a human skull buried in the bank,
and named it so? Or was the creek's
own shape a skeletal elbow curving
around a bend into a shoulder,
or a knee swelling to the width of
a thigh bone? Whatever idea joined itself
to this slip of water snaking through
the wheat and intersecting my own
by-pass into town, it knocked at my mind,
un-fleshed, chill, chalky, hard.

Persistent. A week later it flashes at me
as I undress — the bathroom mirror, silver
as the stream. My hip-bones watching me.
The contour of the ivory beneath the skin
of my own forehead, surfacing.

Overleaf

After a breathless dawn the wind blows free,
upturns the silver poplar leaves. They glance,
pale faces, restless, up and down the tree.
Like poplar leaves, the words within me dance,
but does some secret hope pervade my heart?
And might I be content for youth to play its part,
then reach its nadir at the end of Fall?

Perhaps my words glisten against their will.
Soon, will their transient luster turn to yellow —
a gold, translucent foil — enough to fill
the cracks of footpath, hill, and rocky hollow?
Come Fall, word-weary minds dream of recess —
the lightness, and the light, of leaflessness.

Materfamilias

Mother tree,
bald, ancient,
with shoulders white
as bleached bones,
you are still green
as a young girl
where mosses velvet
your south, and life
tufts some of
your knotted fingers.
You cup small jays
in your elbows,
wrinkle your brown skin
to shelter larvae,
and your roots
beam and buttress
marmot burrows.

Today, though
the morning mountain
holds its breath,
you bend
to an eternal gale.
You are a signal
to weather, a signpost
in time, pointing
the way the wind went.

Mobile

Freed by a nomad wind,
all afternoon the aspen leaves,
like grown children,
leave home. The color of

moonrise, they drift
and eddy on the twilight
mirrors, on those pools of light
where the stream conserves itself

at the end of a dry season.
Changelings, the yellow hearts
swim on the brim
between world and stars

in a brief, giddy autonomy.
Tonight the first
frost will lock around them
its slow, cold fingers.

Golden Delicious

Last night's killing frost uncolored
the whole of the Skagit. This afternoon,
hiking the valley, I found
a spread of apple trees gone wild —
black nets of branches
heavy with yellow fruit, frozen
solid enough to last the winter.

If the freeze had held them
in its hand, vise-hard, not let go . . .

But a rogue river of wind, come loose
from the Sound at noon, began
to thaw the valley rotten.
Now the numbed apples are falling,
one, one, one, till the gray ground boils
with bruised gold, hanging the old orchard's
autumn air with the winy smell of loss.

M. C. Escher's Three Worlds

The leaves — we recognize beech, birch, oak, maple
    — all dead,
float thinly on the silver cheek of the lake, film its
alien skin with pale freckles, mark a glass floor,

a boundary stilled in time by a dead artist.
    Underneath —
like a porcelain inlay — the round-eyed carp has
lurked for decades in the water's dark enamel

which, by some magic, is lucid enough to accept
    light and
hold it on paper. Rooting in the water mirror, the bare
branches are only abstractions of themselves

at two removes, recognizable but reversed, a
    platonic idea
of trees. The top rim of this rendering we discern
as the bottom of the real, guessing that for Escher

actual elms stretched up from there, on an edge
    of land
fictional for us except as probability. Really,
the fish, tensed like a question mark, in ambush

between the scrim of leaves and shadow-branches, is
    the only
live thing in these monochrome worlds. And even it
waits motionless within the print, like some

curious paperweight object suspended in acrylic,
    preserved
in its long, upward observation of our otherness, as if
inquiring: Do you, too, define yourselves as part

of some creator's dream? Are you veiled in
    questions,
leaf-lapped, tangled in eternal twilight by
intimations of celestial trees?

Behind the walls

On this street our new house
is going up among the trees,
the open air of Bellingham
boxed in, closed off
from rain, birds, light, leaves.
Here, day by day, is a new
kind of space — defined by
upright beams of pine,
narrow yellow in the morning's sun,
sentenced to a long darkness.

Months from now, when it is all done,
others may notice siding,
shutters, the color of paint,
but I'll be dreaming of
the secret trees behind the walls
standing straight and strong
as pines in the free groves outside.

What the wind can do

Twilight. With darkness coming on
through the open door, I am losing more and more
of the gold. From the field next to the barn
a fog spreads over the house, taut and clean as a bedsheet,
a blotter. Light still falls from the height
but in particles, the way pollen drops to the hand
under an open sunflower.

Then, like a sigh, the night opens its mouth, breathes.
With fog sliding north on this sled of air, a new dime
of light appears like an offering, a lost coin just found,
over a horizon liquid with trees beginning to sway.
Even the dirt road glistens like a river. Oat fields tilt,
undulate under the kneading air, a Welsh green, the stalks
splinters of moon, the body of night a dancing silver.

To a Winter Chestnut: Five Haiku

For Madeleine

Behind me, a thud
on the sidewalk, padded with
leaves like yellow hands.

I turned. It was like
a key. The jade husk unlocked,
birthing you at my feet.

New as a baby,
you held the heavy secrets
of chestnut trees.

Now fingered and shrunk,
your Fall gloss faded, you look
worn out. But it's near

Christmas, and still you
ride my pocket — Christ's coal for
my five cold fingers.

I gave this day to God

I gave this day to God when I got up, and look,
look what it birthed! There, up the hill, was

the apple tree, bronze leaves, its fallen apples
spilling richly down the slope, the way God spilled

his seed into Mary, into us. In her the holy promise
came to rest in generous soil after a long

fall. How often it ends in gravel, or dry dust.
Blackberry patches thorny with distraction. Oh,

I pray my soul will welcome always that small
seed. That I will hail it when it enters me.

I don't mind being grit, soil, dirt, mud-brown,
laced with the rot of old leaves, if only the seed

can find me, find a home and bear a fruit
sweet, flushed, full-fleshed — a glory apple.

Acknowledgments

Grateful acknowledgment is made to the editors of the following publications, in which some of these poems first appeared:

The Best Spiritual Writing of 1998 (Harper SanFrancisco, 1998): "Rising: The Underground Tree"

Books & Culture: "I gave this day to God"

The Christian Century: "What secret purple wisdom," "What the wind can do," "Bone Creek"

Christianity & Literature: "Imprints: Lindisfarne"

Christianity & the Arts: "Benediction: Opening the Summer Cottage"

Crux: "Three Haiku: Queen Anne's Lace," "I begin to understand how weather"

First Things: "Flathead Lake, Montana," "Weather Forecast: Prolonged Dry Period"

Image: "Folio"

Kinesis: "The Writing on the Rock"

Perspectives: "The Herb Garden"

South Coast Poetry Journal: "Edges of Wales"

The Sow's Ear: "M. C. Escher's Three Worlds"

The poems "Bare roofs" and "The Meaning of White Oaks" (originally "The meaning of oaks I") were published in *The Sighting* (Shaw, 1981).

The poems "April," "How to paint a promise in January," "Heart Spring" (originally "New Birth: Heart Spring"), "Highway Song for Valentine's Day," "Spring song, very early morning," "In my living room," "A Song for Simplicity," "Raspberries," "Grass" (originally ". . . but the word of our God will stand forever"), "Harvesting" (originally "Hundredfold"), "Materfamilias," "To a Winter Chestnut: Five Haiku," and "Behind the walls" were published in *Polishing the Petoskey Stone* (Shaw, 1990).

The poems "Edges of Wales," "I begin to understand how weather," "Stigmata," "Three Haiku: Queen Anne's Lace," "On the river bank, Bibury," "Diamonds that leap," "Evaporation," "Golden Delicious," "Mobile," and "M. C. Escher's Three Worlds" were published in *Writing the River* (Piñon Press, 1994; revised edition by Regent College Publishing, 1998).

The poems "Enthusiasm: The Woods in Spring," "What secret purple wisdom," "Rising: The Underground Tree," "Benediction: Opening the Summer Cottage," "Windy," "Flathead Lake, Montana," "Imprints: Lindisfarne," "Weather Forecast: Prolonged Dry Period," "Folio," "The Writing on the Rock," and "What the wind can do" were published in *The Angles of Light* (Shaw, 2000).

The poem "Stigmata" was included in the anthology *Alive to God*, a Festschrift in honor of Dr. James Houston, edited by J. I. Packer and Loren Wilkinson (InterVarsity, 1992).

The poem "Golden Delicious" was included in the anthology *Odd Angles of Heaven*, edited by David Craig and Janet McCann (Shaw, 1994).

The poem "I gave this day to God" was quoted in *The NIV Application Commentary on Ecclesiastes and Song of Songs* by Iain Provan (Zondervan, 2001).